Hands-On Faith

FAMILY FUN

How to Excite, Fascinate, and Wow
Your Kids with the Principles of God

by Janet Lynn Mitchell

Carson-Dellosa Christian Publishing
Greensboro, North Carolina

It is the mission of Carson-Dellosa Christian Publishing to create the highest-quality Scripture-based children's products that teach the Word of God, share His love and goodness, assist in faith development, and glorify His Son, Jesus Christ.

". . . teach me your ways so I may know you. . . ."
Exodus 33:13

Credits

Author: Janet Lynn Mitchell
Editor: Lisa Reed
Illustrator: Julie Anderson
Layout Design: Mark Conrad
Cover Design: Annette Hollister-Papp
   © 2004 Dynamic Graphics & © IT Stock

DEDICATION

This book is dedicated to my children, Jenna, Jason, and Joel. For they have taught me the true meaning of family fun—it is spending time with those you love.

ACKNOWLEDGMENTS

Special thanks to the members of my writers critique group, Char Derby, Patricia Evans, Bonnie Compton Hanson, Marilyn Jaskulke, Karen Kosman, Joanne Schulte, Beverly Bush Smith, and Suzan Strader for their constant encouragement, words of wisdom, and contributions to this book. They are all true examples of hands-on faith.

Table of Contents

Introduction to the Hands-On Faith Series

A Parent's Charge from the Lord (Deuteronomy 6:5-9)

Love the LORD your God with all your heart and with all your soul and with all your strength. These commandments that I give you today are to be upon your hearts. Impress them on your children. Talk about them when you sit at home and when you walk along the road, when you lie down and when you get up. Tie them as symbols on your hands and bind them on your foreheads. Write them on the doorframes of your houses and on your gates.

As I read these words in my Bible, I realized that it was my job as a parent to impress the commandments upon my children. I discovered the word *impress* means to make a distinctive mark, to excite, fascinate, and wow my children. Using techniques and ideas from my teaching experiences and my own imagination, I began to implement these principles and teach my children faith in Jesus Christ.

The Hands-On Faith series is written for parents who are seeking to make an impact in their children's lives. Foster parents, grandparents, even aunts and uncles can discover ways in which they can participate in family fun. Whatever the makeup of a family, the Hands-On Faith series teaches that every Christian family has a holy purpose; God has a plan in mind for each of them.

Family Fun draws families together. Through its humorous and upbeat style, this book will encourage your family to:

- love, honor, and serve God.
- have all family members come to know Jesus as their Savior.
- develop a strong sense of family unity.
- experience joy, have fun together, and laugh together.
- provide a structured time each week for the family to come together for sharing, prayer, and worship.

Hands-On Faith: Family Fun

Through show-and-tell, *Family Fun* includes practical, fun, and challenging activities parents can use to reinforce family relationships and faith in Christ. This book uses examples by real families who have dared to create a home full of laughter.

It demonstrates ways in which families can celebrate their faith throughout the day and provides realistic tips for families dealing with life's tough moments. From creating a home of laughter, outrageous activities to try, and fun ways to worship—your family will experience family fun.

Chapter One
Creating a Home Full of Laughter

It's been said that a family who plays together stays together. Yes, family fun is essential and a key ingredient in bringing and keeping families together. Through it, parents often forget their worries and children thrive, realizing they are valued.

Fun does not have to be expensive. It simply means giving your children your full and undivided attention. Through playtime and fun, children open up and let their parents into their world. A father shooting baskets with his son is likely to learn more about his child's day than a father quizzing him before bedtime. Through play and fun, you are given teachable moments that could result in lifetime lessons for our children.

"So how do we create a home full of laughter?" you may ask. "How do we create a home where joy is present and Christ is honored?"

Years ago, my husband Marty, and I, along with our children Jenna, Jason, and Joel—weren't having fun. The challenges in our lives ran longer than my grocery list. With Joel born prematurely and requiring life support; Jenna, our oldest at age six, diagnosed with juvenile diabetes and thirteen hospitalizations within one year; Uncle Rusty in a tank in Iraq; the death of my grandparents; the aerospace layoffs where Marty worked for years; and our car accident; we braced ourselves daily for the next "whatever."

As overwhelmed as we were, somehow, someway, Marty and I had to bring laughter back into our home. Determined, I went out and bought an engraved, wooden sign and hung it in the entry way of our home. It boldly declared our new goals: "Live Well, Laugh Often, and Love Much."

I knew that for Christians, living well required trusting God with those things that were out of our control. It meant making the best of each day and honoring God by the way we lived.

Laughing often was a conscious decision. We began to look for opportunities to do so and for ways in which humor could be expressed. There was no more crying over spilled milk. Our new motto was, "If it won't matter in ten years, it's not a problem; it's an inconvenience." And we all know that an inconvenience is just that, an inconvenience—not a true life problem.

Loving much came naturally. We consciously began to teach our children how to express this love. Life had become precious and not one day went by without my children being told, "I love you." Our children have since grown. Now, with Jenna at nineteen, Jason seventeen, and Joel a healthy thirteen-year-old, they know how to express love. They have learned that, even in the midst of their peers, it's cool to offer their grandparents a hug.

Living well, laughing often, and loving much taught us that we could have fun despite the crisis at hand. We learned that as parents we could create a home of laughter and that a family who determines to have fun can do just that. Joy, a positive attitude, and a touch of humor were three attributes we embraced while creating a home full of laughter. Together they provided us a new perspective and reminded us to live well.

A Touch of Humor

Humor defuses the difficult, making it dealable. Helping our children find humor and see the funny, lighthearted side of things, we can turn a defeatist attitude into one of perseverance. This can move children beyond disappointment and provide a balance where needed. Even though one's heart may ache, it is possible to chuckle, giggle, and convulse with laughter. Laughter gives a person the power to endure, to rise up, to move mountains, and to climb through life's most difficult situations.

Become a comedian and learn a few clean knee-slappers by checking out the website www.prongo.com. This site contains over 500 jokes to peruse. Watch funny movies, play games, and most of all, find humor where you least expect it.

Yes, parents do have the choice to create a home where laughter is a second language. Laughter is contagious, and once it bares roots in your home, your family will experience blessings beyond measure. Laughter will make your family fun.

Your decision is made. You too will want your family to live well, laugh often, and love much. By experiencing joy, maintaining a positive outlook, and finding a touch of humor, the tone in your home is set.

A Positive Look

We can teach our children to have fun through the good and even the bad and difficult times of their lives. We can show them how to look on the bright side of things—how to turn lemons into lemonade and see their glass half full instead of half empty. Just as we teach them how to brush their teeth, parents can teach and nurture optimism. We can show them how to turn negatives into positives. We can teach our children how to laugh at situations, and at times— even themselves.

Words have power. Instead of allowing our children to say, "I can't," have them say, "I'll try." Then celebrate their efforts and praise their attempts. Our reactions and responses set the pace and tone in our homes. We lead the way, and our children are sure to observe and likely to follow our examples. Yes, as parents we can demonstrate what it is to *"give thanks in all circumstances, for this is God's will for you in Christ Jesus."* according to 1 Thessalonians 5:18.

 ## Experiencing Joy

Ultimate joy is experiencing an intimate relationship with Jesus Christ. It is Christ dwelling within us who brings joy, thus establishing the tone and atmosphere in our homes.

Nehemiah 8:10 states, ". . .*for the joy of the LORD is your strength.*" The joy we receive from knowing, celebrating, and living out our faith will be the strength, energy, backbone, stability, and excitement experienced in our families.

Creating a home full of laughter was a goal of the Israelites. In the Old Testament we read about how they worshiped, celebrated, and praised. And we see how they affirmed their faith—declaring the attributes of God in the presences of others. Their goals were always before them as they went about their lives honoring God and following the instructions of Deuteronomy 6:9: "*Write* [the commandments] *on the doorframes of your houses and on your gates.*"

Chapter Two
Fun Things to Do

Your family is ready to have some serious fun—so what do you do? What activities might delight your young ones, not bore your teens, and wouldn't require a recreational leader from the YMCA?

The possibilities are as vast as your imagination. They're determined by your family's likes, needs, and desires. Every idea mentioned in this book can be adapted to fit your family's style. While reading, use your creativity and jot down additional fun ideas that come to mind. Then break out of your norm. Try an idea that seems a tad outrageous. For example, buy a hundred balloons and see what fun they can be!

♥ Celebrate the Day

How do you change a humdrum day into one filled with excitement and fun? What can you do to put the sparkle back into the eyes of a child who's been in bed all week with a broken leg? How can you surprise Mom knowing you'll get a smile in return? Filling a closet, bedroom, or bathroom with balloons is a sure way to get your family laughing. Better yet, involve your children.

Have them blow up the balloons as you tie the knots. Then when Dad is sleeping, pack his car with balloons of all colors. Add a note declaring your love and giggle quietly as you wait for Dad's great discovery.

Grab a Pen

Find out the name and address of a missionary family supported by your church or local ministry. Gather your family together and write this missionary family a letter. Involve your younger children by having them draw pictures to accompany the letter. Look on a globe or map and discover where this family lives. Pray over the letter, and ask God to use this family for His glory. This activity will not only bless and encourage the missionary family, but it will help your children see beyond their community and be a part of the worldwide body of Christ.

 Create a Family Night

Thirteen years ago, our family took the plunge and began a weekly family night. It was one night when we said no to all other activities and spent it with our family—for our family. "So what's a family night?" you ask. "What makes this night any different from any other night of the week?"

For us, family nights are nights when we gather together for fun with a purpose. They are a time to instill our Christian beliefs and values in our children. They've become a tool that's helped us provide our children with a biblical foundation. They are times we've committed to them, offering affirmation, guidance, communication, acceptance, encouragement, and understanding. Family nights are when we help our children realize the whys behind our choices, behaviors, and priorities. On a family night, we share, worship, and pray together. We play games, laugh, and celebrate being a family.

We believe that every family that takes the challenge of creating a weekly family night is headed for an awesome experience. Just as He did for us, God will show up and your family will be blessed beyond your imaginations.

Plan Your Life

According to Psalm 118:24, each day is a day our Lord has made. We are to rejoice and be glad in it. We can teach our children that every day is precious and a gift from God. We can help them foresee future events and share in the excitement of life. Purchasing or making a large family calendar is a great way to teach children the value of how we spend our time and involve them in scheduling events.

For younger children, the larger the calendar the better. Drawing pictures can replace written words, thus making the calendar readable by all. If you plan to go on a family vacation to the beach, have your children draw a picture of the packed van. On several days before the trip, fill the calendar with stickers or pictures of starfish, the ocean, and even a milk shake or two. Help your child prepare for his dentist appointment by drawing a big tooth on the calendar. Anticipate birthdays by coloring a present or balloons.

For your teens, a family calendar is vital. Undoubtedly it's obvious to all that your family is headed in several directions. A family night must be scheduled or it may not happen. Teens appreciate knowing ahead of time when Dad will be gone on a business trip and when Mom has that important meeting. Parents, on the other hand, need to know the dates and times of children's games, church events, and slumber parties. I believe families who plan together and manage their time are able to make time for each other and most importantly God.

♥ Dig Up the Past

Go on a hunt and dig out old photos of you and your spouse as children and teenagers. Look for any letters or memorabilia from your past and gather your family together to share stories from those days. Talk about how times have changed and how they have stayed the same. Fill in the blanks and answer these sample questions as your children listen to your stories of the past.

• When I was young, _____ was considered "cool."

• My favorite subject in school was _____.

• The thoughts I had as a teen that kept me awake were _____.

• My favorite television show was _____.

• I once had a pet named _____.

• One of my greatest memories from high school is_____.

♥ If I Had a Million Dollars

Find some old magazines and a few pair of scissors. Have your entire family go through the magazines cutting out pictures of items they would like to purchase if they had a million dollars. Collage these pictures onto a large sheet of construction paper. Have each family member share what items they would purchase and why. Listen as your family shares dreams and uses their imaginations. Talk about what things are important to you and your family. Lastly, remind your children that their salvation is free—yet its cost was great.

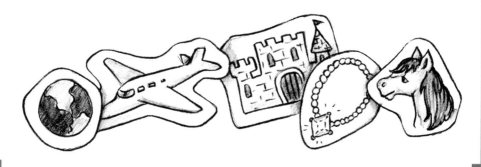

Hector the Collector

It is possible to model responsibility, enforce daily chores, and even have some fun while doing these things. Playing Hector the Collector has given many families a simple way to keep a neat and tidy home. Deem one member of your family to be Hector for the week.

Playing Hector the Collector will aid in teaching your children to take responsibility for their personal items. Each night, just before bedtime, Hector will do his duty as he walks through your home collecting all the left out, misplaced items forgotten by your family. Hector will then place these items in a box or laundry basket. Depending upon the rules and consequences your family creates, family members may have to pay a quarter for every item they wish to redeem, or do an extra family chore in exchange for their math homework, beloved stuffed bunny, or other item they failed to put away. Just remember to pick up your shoes as you head for bed or you, too, may find yourself cleaning the dishes.

Make a Trade

How about a weekend without TV, video games, and computers? Instead, fill it with bike rides, skating, baseball, and an old-fashioned game of charades. Grab your chalk and challenge your children to a game of hopscotch. Break out the hula hoop and show your family how it's done. Build a fire pit and or buy a hibachi. Sit around the "campfire" roasting marshmallows and make s'mores. Videotape the highlights of your weekend and save the tape for the moment your child dares to say, "Dad, Mom, I'm bored!"

A Love for Country

Instilling a love for country is a gift that we can give our children. But how do we instill this precious gift? How do we show our pride in our country and raise patriotic children?

From an early age, parents can teach their children about the wonderful country in which they live. Parents can help them to understand the history and traditions that their country treasures.

Listed below are a few hands-on ways in which your family can show God their gratitude for the homeland He has given them.

- Display your flag on holidays or every day of the week. Learn about its colors, symbols, and what each represents. Teach your children "flag etiquette" and the respect that it deserves.

- Discover what historical events have taken place in your hometown. Go to these locations and take a few pictures. Conduct a search on the Internet for national parks and read all you can about the site. The website www.historyplace.com is a superb resource for American history. It also offers a collection of speeches and homework help.

- Discover your roots. Find out what country your ancestors came from. Learn why and how they left their homes and ventured to a new land. What prices did they have to pay for this newfound freedom and opportunities? How have their sacrifices affected your lives? Through discovering our family roots, we were amazed to find out that my great-grandfather came to the United States by tremendous sacrifice and yet with great expectations. He was only fourteen-years-old when his family smuggled him out of his country before making the fourteen day voyage. For his own protection, he dressed as a young girl—finding his way to the United States. What odds have we faced, risks have we taken, and sacrifices have we made? What are we doing to create better lives for our great-grandchildren and their children? We must remember that a Christian heritage will not happen by accident, and that despite the heritage that was or was not passed down to us, we are in the position to create change for the future.

- Purchase puzzles that depict pictures of national parks or monuments. Locate information pertaining to these places and share it with your children while you race to see who will put the last piece of the puzzle in place.

- Learn a few patriotic songs. Rehearse your national anthem and sing with gusto!

- Read the history of your country. Go to the library, or search the Internet and discover the Christian principles on which your nation was established. Read about its heroes and famous forefathers. For those living in the United States, books such as *America's Providential History* by Mark A. Beliles and Stephen K. McDowell tell stories your children most likely will not hear in school. It tells of colonies that observed days of fasting and prayer and soldiers who knelt to pray on battlefields. It tells of a nation founded by God-fearing people and established by prayer.

- Help your children to recognize your nation's public officials, past and present. Talk about their duties and great responsibilities. Take a few moments to pray for your current leaders. Look up their names and addresses on the Internet or in your local telephone book. Encourage your children to write them a note letting them know that you have prayed for them. Most likely, they will, in return, send your family a letter of thanks. Remember to include these leaders in your family prayers—whether or not you agree with their political viewpoints. When our children were young, I wrote the following prayer. It was a great way for my family to pray for our country. I pray it will also be helpful to yours.

Dear God,

We thank You for our country—the home of the brave and free.
We thank You for its comforts and its beauty that we see.
We ask that You would bless it and all our leaders too.
We ask that Your will be done in all that we say and do. Amen.

- Find family members or friends who have served in the military. Ask them to share with you and your family some of the experiences they had while defending their country. Follow up by having your children make and send them a thank-you card. Remember to pray for these servicemen, their families, and those who are actively serving your country.

I've Got a Dream

What dreams do your children have? How could your family help to cultivate them or encourage their birth? God often places big dreams into the hearts of our children. From creating a business—selling lemonade on a warm day—to a child's great invention, parents can foster dreams and help them to become a reality.

God often uses children to bring about remarkable outcomes. From the story in John chapter six of the boy who gave Jesus his lunch to eight-year-old Josiah who was crowned king of Jerusalem (2 Kings 22), children can make a mark for the Lord.

We too, can teach our children that when they offer their talents, abilities, personalities, and kindness to God, God in turn, uses it in mighty ways.

Joel 2:28 reminds us that God is the creator of dreams as it states, *"And afterward, I will pour out my Spirit on all people. Your sons and daughters will prophesy, your old men will dream dreams, your young men will see visions."*

How do we communicate to our children that it's more than okay to dream big? How do we respond to them when they tell us of their latest invention or idea? Do we help them try to fulfill their dream and encourage them to go for it? What do we do when their aspirations don't match their size and ability? Do we sit back, and as with David, watch them gather five smooth stones and conquer their giant (1 Samuel 17:40, 49-50)? Do we cheer them on and partner with them helping to make their dreams a reality?

"What can I do to help?" Joel, my ten-year-old son, asked. The shocking news of September 11, 2001, spread fast—even to ears thought too young to comprehend. But Joel did understand. He knew that his nation was wounded and that many lives had been changed forever.

"But, really Mom, what can I do? What can I do to help those families?"

"Joel, you can pray. You know, praying is probably the most powerful thing you can do."

"Mom, I've already prayed, and more than one time a day! I want to know what my hands can do to help."

I was now thinking on overload. I had no idea what a ten-year-old could do to help this situation, much less use his hands to do it. I added to my prayer list—"An idea for Joel so that he can help victims of September 11."

A day later, the thought came. "Joel, I've got it! Do you remember the beaded cross pin that you made at camp a couple of summers ago?"

"The one that was made with safety pins?" Joel asked.

"Yes. Why can't you try to design an American flag? You know stringing red, white, and blue beads onto safety pins. Then maybe you could collect donations to help the victims' families."

Off to the craft store we went, buying each and every pack of

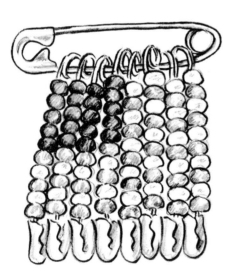

red, white, and blue beads that we could find. Feeling as if we were on a scavenger hunt, we shopped for and bought safety pins—seventeen thousand safety pins to be exact. Joel named his project Helping Hands, and even found some friends who were willing to help assemble the flag pins. Joel then made signs that boldly read, "My Gift to You When You Donate to the Red Cross." Within just a few weeks, Joel had managed to collect $5,000 in donations.

After such an overwhelming task, Joel's hands were tired. They had not yet recovered from accidental pokes from the sharp points of the pin when he heard the horrific news—a postal worker had died from anthrax.

Again, questions came flying. "Mom, what is anthrax? How did it get there? Aren't the postmen and women scared?"

I answered each question to the best of my knowledge. But then came a question I had no answer for. "Mom, what's the name of our postman?"

A lump formed in my throat as I realized that we had lived in our home for ten years, and I had no idea who delivered our mail each day.

"Do you think our postman is scared?" Joel asked.

The next afternoon Joel stood next to our mailbox, singing to himself until he saw the wheels of the U.S. mail truck. With a smile, he introduced himself to the mail carrier.

"Hi, I'm Joel. I live here."

"Glad to meet you, Joel. My name's Jimmy."

"Are ya scared?"

"Scared?"

"Yeah, about the anthrax."

"We're doing our jobs, and we're being extra careful. Thanks for asking," Jimmy said just before he drove away.

I heard the door shut with gusto. "Mom!" Joel shouted. "His name is Jimmy! Our mailman's name is Jimmy!"

Within seconds, Joel met me in the kitchen. "I want to do more. Mom, I want to do something for Jimmy. Just how many friends at the post office do you think Jimmy has?"

"Maybe twenty?" I guessed. Two hundred and five was the official number of postal workers in our city.

Again, Joel and I went to the craft stores, buying every red, white, and blue bead we found. Due to a shortage of safety pins, we made calls, buying pins directly from the manufacturer. Joel rehung his sign, and Helping Hands was back in business.

This time it was different. Joel was not collecting donations. He was making gifts of encouragement—a flag pin for every postal worker of Orange, California. After completing his task, Joel typed a note and printed it out two hundred and five times.

"I have made you this flag pin to remind you that people in our city appreciate the work you do for us. I am praying for you as you deliver our mail. I know that God will bless America! Love, Joel."

It was while Joel was attaching the notes to the flag pins that Allison, a neighborhood friend of Joel's stopped by. "Hey, can I help?" she asked.

"Yeah. You're just in time. I want to get these in the mailbox before the mailman comes."

Joel handed Allison a pen and she began signing her name to the notes. Sitting side-by-side, they worked until each flag pin was accompanied by a note. They then boxed up the flag pins, tied a bow around them, and added a card that read, "To: Jimmy and Friends." They placed the package in our mailbox, and raised the red flag. With a task well done, Joel and Allison went off to play. It was not until later that afternoon that I got the call.

"Hi, are you Joel's mom?" the voice asked.

"Yes," I answered.

"Well, you must be very proud of your son. I am the Postmaster in Orange, and I'd like to know if you would bring Joel and Allison to the post office tomorrow morning about 9:00. I thought it would be great if they themselves could pass out the flag pins to the mail carriers."

The next morning came. The Postmaster divided the 205 postal workers into three groups. Three times Joel and Allison took front stage encouraging the mail carriers and handing out pins.

Tears gathered in some of the postal workers' eyes as they received their pins from Joel and Allison. "I think it's fantastic that you two took the time to do this and came to talk to us," one man said while shaking Joel's hand. Others offered hugs and words of thanks. Before the morning was over, Joel and Allison were made honorary mail carriers of Orange, California.

Through this experience Joel taught me many lessons. I learned that the only requirements needed to help another are a set of helping hands and a willing heart. Allison has reminded me, that when my fingers are cracked and tender—it's time for me to call on a friend. Through the lives of two ten-year-olds, I am now assured that each of us can do something to help our nation heal. From saying a prayer for those who pass you by, writing a letter to an unknown serviceman, or stringing small beads, these gifts of time deeply affect those they touch.

"But, really Mom, what can I do? What can my hands do to help?" Joel asked.

I am proud of my son for dreaming big dreams and believing that God could use his two hands to touch the lives of those he's never met.

God will use your child's hands. Have your children share their dreams with your family. Discuss ways in which your family can encourage, partner, and become birthing coaches to your child's dreams. Be prepared for the incredible exhilaration as your family lifts their hands to God, offering your dreams to Him—for His glory.

Chapter Three
Fun Places to Go

Sometimes a change of environment is just what a family needs. A family vacation or even a few hours away from home, the phone, laundry, and chores yet to be done, can provide the perfect opportunity to get away from it all and focus on each other.

Before taking an airplane trip, I've made each of my children goodie bags consisting of a card game, crayons, paper, granola bars, fruit snacks, and a new book. I also packed hand-held CD and tape players with headsets, Christian music tapes, and the latest Bible story cassette.

If you're planning a trip, locate information about the places you expect to visit. Write to city and state tourist offices and request all the information they have pertaining to the cities you will pass through or your chosen destination. Sit down with your children and share this information with them. Get out a map and chart your trip. Allow the children to help pack their bags and not to forget their friends' addresses so that they can send a postcard saying, "Having a great time, wish you were here!"

Car trips, no matter the distance, do at times get tedious. One summer our family drove through Nebraska. At first the sighting of cows and corn fields thrilled the children. In fact the first day or so they tried to count the cows they saw. However, this thrill soon died and one of the children said with a sigh, "Mom, one can only count so many cows."

Road Tested Car Games

Traveling with children can be most exciting. Whether it's a car ride, a bumpy trip in a motor home, or hours on a plane, children get restless and eventually ask, "How much longer? Just when are we going to get there?"

Marty's and my motto has always been, "Half the fun is getting there." It did not take long to convince our children of this truth. It did, however, require a little effort and advance preparation in order for this fun to take place.

The games listed in this chapter have been proven by my family to be fun, and most can be played while in a car, plane, train, or even at home sitting in one's family room. Be prepared to laugh, hum, guess the outrageous, and even go out of your way seeking that long-lost letter of the alphabet.

- **Twenty Questions** is a game that can be played by all. One of your family members thinks of "something" that they have seen or heard. He then tells the other players if their "something" is a Bible character, cartoon character, animal, song, or person. The players then ask questions that can be answered by a yes or a no, hoping that by the process of elimination they can figure out what the "something" is. The players have a maximum of twenty questions they can ask but can guess at any time. Whoever guesses the correct answer wins, and then it's their turn to choose that special "something," and the game continues.

- **I Spy** is one of our favorite games. One family member chooses an object. For example, a red button on a jacket. She then says, "I spy with my own eyes something red." The other players then take turns looking around and guessing what the object may be. The family member who guesses the object correctly gets to be the next "spy" and the game continues.

- **Name that Tune** is a great game. It doesn't matter whether or not your family is musically inclined, they can still hum or whistle a tune and have some fun. To play Name that Tune, one of your family members hums or whistles a few notes of a song and the others try to guess what song it is. If no one recognizes the song, the hummer or whistler adds a few extra measures of the song, and the guessing goes on. The first person to guess correctly becomes the next to choose a song and hum the tune.

- **Alphabet Autobahn** is a race from A to Z. Your family works together to find and call out letters from the alphabet in order. These letters can be found on car license plates, billboards, highway signs, and even bumper stickers. Through laughter you may find yourselves passing cars just so you can check out a license plate seeking the next needed letter.

Yes, once you've played along, you too will see that half the fun in traveling is the fun you have along the way.

Ready, Set, Go

Fun can happen when we least expect it. Being prepared makes these unexpected moments more enjoyable. For the parent on the go, I suggest packing a picnic basket and placing it in the trunk of your car so that it's ready to be used at a moments notice. Consider keeping these items on hand:

A pad of paper
Sunscreen
Brush or comb
Plastic silverware
Paper towels
Deck of playing cards
Games

Frisbee®
Antibacterial or baby wipes
Granola bar or other snack
Markers and pencils
Bottled water
Large blanket
First aid kit

Having these items available allows you to stop by a park and let the children play for fifteen minutes. They provide something to do when time is crawling by. You can occasionally rotate the games—making sure your basket is always full of surprises.

Family Camp

One of my family's favorite places to go is family camp. For the first ten to fifteen summers of our children's lives, we packed the van and headed to Forest Home Christian Conference Center in Forest Falls, California. There, we had a fun-filled vacation playing together, learning together, and spending time as a family. We grew in our faith, were refreshed, and challenged to live our lives for Christ.

Unlike a trip to Walt Disney World®, where you do all the planning, most family camps held at Christian Conference Centers ask that you show up and they do the rest. Programs are designed for the family. Children, teens, and parents—single or married, can find something they enjoy. Grandma and Grandpa can even go along. Whether or not they feel like hiking, playing horseshoes, or tug-of-war, they can watch their grandchildren and cheer them on.

You, too, can take your family to family camp. Conduct a search on the Internet with the words Christian camping, Christian Conference Center, or check out Forest Home at www.foresthome. org. One week at camp, learning, growing, and being challenged in your faith will exceed the hours that you or your children will spend in Sunday school for an entire year.

At the age of nine, Joel wrote a story about our family's experience at family camp. He then had this story made into a hardbound book. On page 29, get a glimpse of what family camp is all about through the eyes of a young boy.

Forest Home
by Joel Anthony Mitchell

Every summer my family goes to family camp. My mom packs, my dad drives, and I sing all the way. We sleep in cabins. Tanner and Cinnamon, the local bears, know where we live! We eat breakfast, then snack, then lunch, then snack again, then dinner...then we eat French fries and ice cream.

Day camp is the best part. There, I'm with kids my age. We sing, hike, make crafts, and learn more about God. My entire family has "zipped," flying 50 feet over the canyon held up by strong wires, all except my mom who doesn't believe in being high.

At camp I love to golf. My dad, brother, and I golf after almost every meal. In the lake, my dad and I canoe and my sister goes down the 32 foot slide. We visited the craft center making yo-yos, birdhouses, boats, fake snakes, and jewelry.

Every year my family hikes to the prayer chapel and kneels and prays together. God has answered our prayers—even the big one! On the last night of camp, each camper lights a candle representing Christ lighting our world. I love family camp and as far as I can see, the greatest change is the change in me!

♡ All Aboard?

What could be more fun than trying something new? Perhaps something out of the ordinary like a ride on the Pacific, Atlantic, or Transcontinental railroad? When my boys were young they were fascinated with trains. We had a train that circled our Christmas tree. Books about trains filled the boys' night stands, and each of them owned their own conductor's hat, yet neither boy had actually ridden on a real train.

I will never forget the excitement in their voices when my parents called and asked if they could take Marty, the children, and me on a train ride. Our day was wonderful. The boys nodded to the conductor while they filed onto the train. Bright-eyed, they experienced the power of the engine as the train moved along the tracks.

The following Christmas a train rounded our Christmas tree and two boys wearing conductors' hats squealed, "All aboard." Yet, this Christmas was different; the boys knew what it was like to journey down the tracks.

A Night on the Town

Contact your Chamber of Commerce and ask for a list of local and regional events your family could attend. Ask your friends and family about the hot spots in town you have not tried yet. Scan your newspaper and jot down the dates and locations of special events, theatrical performances, and school carnivals. Take a tour of your local government buildings, visit a courthouse, fire station, museum, or radio station. Do a little research and learn about your town's history. Visit its oldest building. Discover how the town got its name and remember to pray for the town's leaders.

A Mini-Vacation

Years ago, my family wanted to get away. Yet finding a time when we were all available was nearly impossible. Juggling baseball games, after-school commitments, and rehearsals for the church musical, we had just a few dates from which to choose.

Finally we did it. We found someone to care for the dog, packed the van, and headed off six miles down the road—for the night. There we checked into a hotel, had a wonderful dinner together, swam in the pool, and played card games into the wee hours of the morning. Sleeping in the following morning was a delight.

Yes, our family found the time to be together that we so desperately needed. Our mini-vacation and dip in the pool is now a treasured memory—one where the phone didn't ring and our family checked in and took the time to check up on one another's lives.

♥ Count the Ways

Ice cream is a popular item in our home. Truthfully, it's not about the ice cream, but about the many creative ways in which we have found to enjoy it. It's about spending time with those we love doing something enjoyable and tasty.

How many different ways has your family found to enjoy ice cream or your favorite food? My family's search for the best ice cream has taken us on a ferry ride to Balboa Island in California. There we savored the famous Balboa ice cream bar dipped in chocolate, wrapped in nuts. Why not venture to a Dairy Queen® for a famous Blizzard®, or visit an old-fashion five and dime and order their specialty? How about buying individual pints of ice cream and then head to the park to eat it—right out of the carton? Do you know how many licks it takes for you or your children to devour a cone stacked three scoops high? Have you taken your family to the newest frozen yogurt store and tried two or three different toppings? Your local ice cream parlor is also a place to visit on a night that needs some extra fun.

Become a Star Gazer

Psalm 147:4 says that God determines the number of the stars and calls them each by name. God asked Abraham to *"Look up at the heavens and count the stars."* (Genesis 15:5) He then promised Abraham that his descendants would be like the stars in the sky—too numerous to count. God also used one single star, the star from the East, to guide the Wise Men to Jesus.

Why not become star gazers? Visit NASA's website at www.NASA. gov and click on the link "For Kids." There you will find awesome pictures, games, and a wealth of information pertaining to stars and our solar system. Why not locate the nearest planetarium and take your family on a day trip? Research stars, planets, and asteroids to learn more about God's universe.

For a family present, purchase a telescope. Locate the planets using a star guide easily found online. If you are unable to access the Internet, head to your local library. Then check out the weather forecast and select the night. Once the sun has set, take your family away from the city lights and the distractions of life. Set up your telescope and watch the stars twinkle or shoot across the sky. If you— like Abraham—try to count the stars, remember that God's blessings for our lives are uncountable and beyond our imaginations.

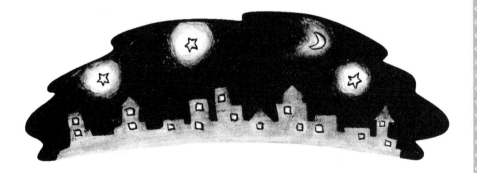

A Camping You Will Go

Surprise your children and dust off the tent. Collect the sleeping bags and head out doors—straight into your own backyard. Once the tent is up or your makeshift tent is created out of beach towels and bed sheets, you will have a night of wonder as you camp under the stars.

While you pretend that you're camping in the Smoky Mountains or over Half Dome in Yosemite National Park, why not:

- Use a flashlight and play a game of nighttime tag.
- Build a campfire with bricks, or use a hibachi.
- Roast hotdogs and marshmallows.
- Drink hot cocoa.
- Instead of playing musical chairs—play musical sleeping bags.
- Sing around the campfire.
- Read a Bible story using a flashlight.
- Study the stars.

Whatever you do while on your camping adventure, pretend that you are far away from the distractions of life. Love your children and have some fun!

A Perfect Sunrise

Check the weather report, then pack your lawn chairs, lay out your jackets, and set the alarm. At just the right time (in the wee hours of the morning), have your family slip out of bed and crawl into your car. Within minutes you will be traveling to your chosen destination. Whether it is to the beach, the top of a hill, or the peak of the highest mountain, you'll still be able to look up and see the dawn breaking. In awe, your family will experience the beauty of the sun rising over the horizon and witness God's handiwork—a miracle for all to enjoy.

Go the Extra Mile

The easiest and most convenient is not always the most exciting. Every once in a while it's just plain fun to go the extra mile and take the long road. For a change, why not take your children to a Christmas tree farm and allow them to hunt for the perfect Christmas tree rather than buying your tree from the local grocery store or dusting off your artificial one? How about taking your children to a pumpkin patch instead of selecting their harvest pumpkins from the produce department at the supermarket? Is there a place fairly close to your home where your family can hike through orchards and pick your own fruit? Find that local apple tree orchard where you can select your own apples, then head home and make caramel apples, apple pie, or apple fritters.

The following account comes from Bonnie Compton Hanson. Here she relives an enjoyable time she spent with her family outdoors.

Open Your Door to Adventure
by Bonnie Compton Hanson

Growing up on a farm, surrounded by woods and mountains, I've always loved the outdoors. Last summer one of my sons, his wife, and two of our grandchildren, Tommy and Andy, decided to meet us at my old family farm and see it for themselves. As we wandered about, my grandsons discovered salt in a streambed, walked up steep gravel roads, toured the old barn, picked wild flowers—just as I had done at their age—and had lots of fun. They also asked umpteen questions, such as, "Grandma Bonnie, were there bears here when you were little?"

I laughed. "No, not bears. But I did see raccoons, possums, wildcats, and mountain lions."

"Wow. Wildcats? Mountain lions. Really?" Tommy and Andy looked around nervously.

Just then a bright yellow kitten from a neighboring farm came bounding toward us across a field. It jumped up into Andy's arms and begged to be petted. He grinned with relief. "Oh, Grandma Bonnie. This must be one of those wild cats you were talking about. Can I keep him?"

There's just one thing keeping you and your family from having fun outdoors, too—your own front or back door. Open it, walk outside, and enjoy one of these 62 tested and inexpensive ways for your family to enjoy each other, bask in the fresh air and sunshine, and get plenty of exercise. Better yet, try them all.

In Your Yard:

1. Play with dandelions (unless you have the perfect lawn). Hold them under someone's chin to see if they like butter—which, of course, everyone does, as the golden blossoms reflect against their skin. You can also carefully split the blossom stem into four of five sections, curl them upward, and float them in a dish. Children can even blow the dandelion's delicate seeds into the air.

2. Create masterpieces on your sidewalk. A box of colored chalk and a lot of enthusiasm combine for a lot of messy fun. Or outline a hopscotch court. Depending on your neighbors and your level of tolerance, you can leave the chalk display up for a few days or hose it right off.

3. Turn your sidewalk into a sports park with toy cars, skates, wagons, scooters, skateboards, and bikes, or trikes. Make sure young children don't go out of your sight. Even older ones need to know their limits and how soon you expect them home.

4. Jump rope. Children can play with individual ropes or one long one turned at each end. Try double dutch!

5. Make a map of your neighborhood. Add the houses of playmates and neighbors. Children can draw cars and trees, or add stickers for them.

6. Swing, slide, and smile. Got a play set or old tire swing? They're great places to play, breathe in the fresh air, and dream.

7. Set up a horseshoe badminton, or croquet set.

8. Set up a bird bath, safely out of your pet's reach.

9. Have an afternoon picnic and laze away under a shady tree.

10. Set up a bird feeder—with seeds for birds or liquid for hummingbirds, or both.

11. Run through the sprinkler's fountain. Glory in its lovely "rainbow." Play musical sprinkler, with one person turning the water on and off and see who gets splashed, as everyone runs around the sprinkler.

12. Cool off in a wading poor or swimming pool. Play Marco Polo. The object of the game is to not get caught by the player Marco. Marco starts on the side opposite the other players. He shouts "Marco" and the others shout "Polo" in an effort not to get caught. The person caught becomes Marco and the game may be started again.

13. Learn how to swim or just float on inner tubes and rest. Always make sure an adult is watching nearby.

14. Collect lots of big boxes, like refrigerator cartons, and let the children go to town building club houses.

15. At night, collect lightning bugs and crickets (while wearing insect repellent, of course.)

16. Look up at the clouds and imagine what each one represents.

17. In the fall, rake leaves and jump into them.

18. Have a parade. Neighbor children can ride their various toys in a parade around the block. Crepe paper, ribbons, or flags make it even more fun.

19. Walk through an upside down world as you splash along a water-covered sidewalk, and see a whole world reflected at your feet.

20. Plant a family garden with a special section for each child. After you describe what kind of growth habits each plant has and how much work each requires, each child can decide what to plant and then be responsible for weeding and watering. One cherry tomato or pumpkin vine per child might be plenty. And, oh, the pride in pointing out, "Look, what I did!"

21. Teach safety with clear instructions for campfires, insects, climbing, and other hazards.

22. Look for a piece of slate to draw and write on.

At a Nearby Park:

23. Take your own wheels (such as bikes, skates, or a skateboard) to zoom around.

24. Take your family pet and play with him.

25. Have a picnic and use a park grill.

26. If you find a small grassy hill, roll down it over and over again.

27. Go fly a kite—especially one you made yourself.

28. Discover how many different kinds of birds you can see and hear.

29. If there's a small pond, check it out for frogs, water lilies, dragonflies, cattails, and fish.

30. Find a place to sail toy boats or float large leaves.

31. If permitted, feed birds, ducks, or squirrels. Be sure to look for regulation signs first.

32. Look for wild flowers. Take their pictures, but don't pick them.

At the Lake or Beach:

33. Use plenty of sunscreen. Take along a cooler and plenty of towels.

34. Teach water safety.

35. Build sand castles.

36. Play with beach balls or Frisbees®.

37. Try out body boards, flotation devices, and inner tubes.

38. Row, row, row, your boat—but wear life vests or other flotation devices and always have an adult along.

39. Look for shells, starfish, and other tide pool creatures—don't touch living ones.

In the Woods:

40. Hike. Wear comfortable tie-up shoes, socks, long pants, insect repellent, and a hat if you're going to be in sunshine. Have bottled water and some first aid supplies with you.

41. See how many kinds of trees you can identify.

42. Teach children to stay away from poison ivy and poison oak.

43. Count how many wild animals you see, such as rabbits, ground squirrels, and lizards. Stay away from snakes or any animal that acts threatened.

44. Pick wild blackberries, dewberries, or huckleberries. Look for nuts. But don't pick berries or nuts you aren't sure about.

45. Collect acorns and pinecones.

46. If you're sure the water is pure, take off your shoes and wade in a small, friendly creek.

47. Look for minnows and dragonflies. Skip stones. Using one pebble, draw on other pebbles.

48. Look for various colored pebbles.

In Your Own Yard:

49. Discover a miniature world at your feet. Encourage your children to squat down or sit and look for as many different bugs, insects, caterpillars, or worms, as possible. List them and try to learn what they eat and their favorite places to live or hang out. You can even do this on a city sidewalk.

50. Follow the trail—an ant trail, that is. Notice how carefully the ants stay to the trail, except when politely passing each other. See if you can track it all the way back to the anthill.

51. Look for four-leaf clovers.

Other Fun Ideas:

In the Winter:

52. Make snow angels.

53. Sled.

54. Go ice-skating.

55. Make snow forts and throw snow balls (but never ice balls.)

Out in the Country:

56. Look for sunflowers, daisies, and other wild flowers.

57. See how many cows, goats, and horses children can count along the road.

58. Look for windmills, silos, grain elevators, and barns.

59. Go horseback riding.

60. Pick watermelons and pumpkins.

61. Pick apples or other fruit.

62. Select a Christmas tree.

Chapter Four
Fun with Family and Friends

Over and over Scripture demonstrates the importance of hospitality and valuing people and not things. Relationships are key to our emotional, social, and spiritual well-being. Friends and family members challenge us to be our best, encourage us when we are down, and as Proverbs 27:17 states, *"As iron sharpens iron, so one man sharpens another."*

Pray and search for other Christian families who have children that blend well with yours. Make it a point to go out together after church, take in a movie, or plan that barbecue you've been pondering. Plan monthly game nights including a devotional or Bible study, and rotate the leadership between the families. Adapt some of the ideas from previous chapters to have fun with family and friends. Make sure that you include laughter and a special snack.

Find time to spend with your extended family and friends. Make a memory, do the unthinkable, and lend a helping hand. As iron sharpens iron—you family will be touched for life.

Make a Memory

A grand idea entered my mind. We somehow needed to lighten the tension that was mounting in our home. Our children needed time with friends and we simply needed to do something fun. I could hardly stifle my giggles as I called two friends and asked if their children (ages 4-6) could come to our family slumber party the following Friday night. The next few days Jenna, (age six), Jason (age four), and I planned our party. We brought down the party box which held odds and ends—party hats, blowers, and napkins from parties of our past. After selecting the perfect video and laying out the sleeping bags, we were set.

Friday night came and so did the children. The pizza was delivered, the video played, and just before the ice cream and bed—it was time. Marty instructed the children to get their jackets and I grabbed the video camera. Marty took half the children in his car and I followed in my van with the other half.

"Where are we going? What are we going to do?" echoed from the backseat.

"Hey, that's my house." Matthew hollered as we drove by and parked around the corner.

"Yes, it is," I said, "and we're about to make it prettier."

Soon the children gathered around Marty and he handed each one their very own roll of toilet paper. "What are we going to do with this?" Matthew asked, obliviously perplexed.

"We're going to decorate. We're going to surprise your mom and dad and wrap your house like a present." Marty then instructed the children to hide or pretend like they were a tree if a car passed by. With shrieks of joy, laughter, and near hysteria, the children papered the house while I videotaped the entire process. Once we finished there, we headed off to house number two making sure that all of our guests were treated alike.

You can only imagine the surprise when our friends found our gift of love spread across their front lawns. I can still hear the giggles the following morning when we brought the children back to clean up the fun they had. And before we left, I handed each of their parents a videotape of our family slumber party and their children pretending to be trees.

You too, can create memories for your children and their friends. If you are not up to decorating your friends' homes, have a family slumber party inviting a few of your children's friends. Play games such as charades, hide and seek, or Junior Outburst™. See which child can build the tallest ice cream sundae. Videotape the fun as your children are certain to watch over and over again a memory they will never forget.

Party with a Purpose

The movie *Titanic* was a hit. Whether children saw it or not, they were all talking about it. I ventured to the store and found several books relating to the voyage and its tragic end. Our family began to research, learning about the people on board and the whys behind the sinking of the ship. We read about many heroes, some even heroes of faith, as they sought to bring others to Christ while floating in the freezing water.

Because the story of the Titanic held many lessons, we decided to have a "party with a purpose." We invited guests and asked them to pretend that our party was to be their first evening on the cruise ship Titanic. They were to pack a small bag of items they wanted to bring, and to dress accordingly, depending upon the social class they chose to represent. The first class would be in formal attire and their food was served on china. Middle class folks dressed as they wished and were free to roam the house. Yet, the lower class wore what they had and were sent to the garage to party. After people felt the impact of the different classes, we opened the house up to all. We also brought out discussion questions and people shared what this small lesson had revealed to them. People also answered the following:

- If you could take three people with you on an ocean voyage, who would they be? Why would you choose these people?

- Show us the most important item you brought and tell us why you brought it.

- Pretend that our ship will sink tomorrow and finish this sentence, "I must _____."

Our party was a huge success and each person left with a photo of herself dressed for the voyage and with a greater understanding of how it feels to be different. Guests also left with a glimpse of what is truly important. Valuable lessons can be found in many movies, especially those intended for families. Don't let these lessons stay at the theaters. Bring them home and help your children apply them to their lives.

♥ Do the Unexpected

We did it. Even though Marty saw it as a great sacrifice, we turned his garage into a game room for our family and friends. Carpeted, adorned with posters and bumper stickers, the garage took on the look of a teen hang out. With a little imagination and the purchase of a pool and a foosball table, which we gave to our children for Christmas, the garage became a game room. Eventually, we hung a television with a video/DVD player from one wall. We found an old refrigerator to hold sodas and dusted off the exercise equipment arranging it accordingly. From playing darts to board games, this room has provided our children a place to hang out through all hours of the day and night. It's drawn children to our home, held pool championships, and contained the laughter of many. As promised, in a few years or so, Marty's garage will return to being his garage.

♡ Helping Hands

Sometimes the most fun we can experience is when we get our eyes off ourselves and focus on others. This is especially helpful when our problems seem so great and our thoughts have turned to trusting ourselves, muttering "oh me" rather than trusting in God.

Why not gather your family and bake cookies for an elderly couple or widow in your church or neighborhood? Why not pick a bouquet of flowers and take them to a convalescent home, giving them to the one who has had few visitors. Plan a movie night and invite the children of a single parent, giving the parent a "night off" and providing the children with fun, fun, and more fun. Design and color posters with words such as, "We Love You," "You are Great", and "Thinking of You" and sneak to place them in the front yard of one who needs a little extra loving.

Caring for others creates a joy from within as God uses our hands to touch the lives of others. And yes, parents do have the power to change the "oh me" into "bless you."

Homebound Missionaries

Why not adopt a college student or two—ones who are away from home and might just need a little extra attention and support? Invite them over and let them experience the joy of family life once again. Cook homemade meals, take them to your church, include them in some family fun, and remember them in your family prayers. Have your children use their imaginations and think of ways they might encourage your newfound friends. A picture mailed, a song sung through the phone, or flowers laid across a place mat may be just the added touch needed—like a hug from God.

Remember that universities are full of international students who would love to spend time in your home. Maybe, just maybe, if your family reaches out, you'll be able to share Jesus with someone who has not heard the Good News. Your children and family are missionaries in your community and one by one you can touch the world.

Come on Over

Clean the house and alert your family to be on their best behavior, as you're inviting the pastor and his family over for dinner. In all reality, relax; this get-together is meant to be a time of fellowship. A pastor knows to expect childlike behavior from children, and has probably experienced an array of humorous situations at the tables of his parishioners. Whatever happens at your home will be no shock to him. In fact, what happens in your home as you gather around your table will most likely affirm your pastor and his family and help establish a relationship between him and your children. Plan a date, pick up the telephone, and place the call.

Go Hunting for Fossils

Have you ever been fossil hunting? Well, the Straders have. Suzan Strader writes, "There are many areas outside of cities that are great for digging. Elementary school children especially love the hunt. Our next-door neighbors, their children and ours, packed picnic baskets, took shovels, old strainers, bottles of water, and buckets and headed for the hills."

Before the fossil hunt, the Straders asked a local park ranger where to dig. "We were surprised to learn that along some canyon roads, right in a local parking lot, there were traces of ancient history waiting to be discovered. Pulling books off the library shelves in advance gave us an idea of how to go about fossil hunting and what to look for. There was great excitement when the first child found a leaf imprinted in a rock. Then another child discovered a few seashells," said Suzan.

"Later on, after lunch, the find of the day was held up by one grubby little hand. Look Mom, a bug! Sure enough, my son had persisted until he uncovered the fossil of an insect. Sharing their discoveries with others made our children aware of another part of God's creation—a part that He hid for just that day."

Ideas for extending your experience:

- Visit a museum of natural history to see what professionals have collected.

- Make quick fossils by pressing leaves, sea shells, or even plastic toy insects into small, smooth mud cakes. Allow them to dry in the sun.

- Gather information on fossils from the Internet.

- Read books on fossils.

- Make a card file collection of facts and drawings to share with others.

Celebrate the Day

Why not call your family and friends, plan a party, and celebrate the unusual. Have you ever partied on Groundhog's Day? Ever planned a party for National Day of Prayer, and topped it off praying for our nation with those you love?

Look through your calendar to get ideas of dates to celebrate. Don't let Grandparents Day pass you by. If Grandma and Grandpa live across the nation, record videos of your family; enjoying the highlights of a simple day. And don't forget to end the videotape with, "Happy Grandparents Day—you're the best!" Why not plan "I'm proud of you" parties, "Way to go!" barbecues, and "Yep, we love you!" celebrations? Instead of a birthday party have a "celebrate life" party; praise, admire, and affirm the honored guest. Learn to think and party outside the box and you'll have a great time celebrating life.

Dad and Daughter Date Night

Dads, why not plan a night and take your daughter on a date? If the dad in your home is not an active part of your daughter's life, ask her grandfather, uncle, or trusted family friend to spend a few hours letting your daughter know how special she truly is. To double the fun, why not go on a double date?

When Jenna was thirteen-years-old, we planned a Dad and Daughter Date Night with ten of her friends and their fathers. Due to the recent death of one girl's father, and a father who wasn't available—Marty escorted three young women on this very special night. Out for dinner they all went. From there, the girls led the "dads" in their lives down the freeway to Palace Park, home of go-carts and laser tag. After their night of fun, each father or special someone gave their daughter or special gal a clear plastic shoe—one that resembled Cinderella's. (These shoes were purchased at a cake decorating store and used to decorate cakes.) A note accompanied each girl's shoe that simply read, "You are beautiful." Six years have gone by and Jenna's special shoe still sits shined and polished on her bedroom shelf. This Dad and Daughter Date Night was truly a night to remember. Dads, why not help the little girl or young woman in your life feel special? Why not put the rest of your world on hold, make a date and:

- Plant flowers.

- Visit a street fair.

- Spend the day at a water park.

- Run barefoot through the rain.

- View the country on horseback.

- Reserve seats at a dinner theater.

- Start your day with a sunrise picnic.

- Go sight-seeing as if you were tourists.

- Hike through the woods and have a picnic.

- Dress in your best and attend a fancy restaurant.

- Surprise her. Meet her after school and walk her home.

- Rent a tandem bicycle and set out for a day of laughter.

- Discover an out of the way café and try a new flavor of latte.

- Teach her how to dance—under the stars in your own backyard.

- Send her a formal invitation and go to a movie premiere.

- Head to a malt shop and browse through your daughter's yearbook or recent photo album.

- Go to the local Christian bookstore and let her pick out a new devotional book.

- Head to the mall and help her find the perfect outfit.

- All in all, don't forget—a father's imprint on a daughter's life lasts forever.

Open Your Doors

Create the home that attracts children. Open your doors and hearts and get to know your children's friends. Having healthy snacks on hand are well worth the investment—and pay high dividends. Once your children and their friends know that they are welcome to hang out, they will come.

Consider yourself missionaries—and take an interest in the lives of these young people. You may be the only adults actively doing so. Know that the children are observing you as role models as you live out your faith before them. Plan a game night and set out various board games on card tables throughout your home. Let them rotate and play from game to game. Break out the karaoke machine and sing with the best of them. Purchase or buy a Dance Revolution pad and a PlayStation®2 game and go at it. Play other games, make caramel apples, and don't forget to pray for these precious children that God has entrusted you to spend time with.

Friends and family members challenge us to be our best, encourage us when we're down and as Proverbs 17:22 states, "*A cheerful heart is good medicine.*"

Hanging Out with the Guys

Most Moms tend to the wash, make sure lunches are made, and have dinner on the table. They hold their ground and insist that bedrooms are tidy, teeth are brushed, and homework is done. Along with these massive duties, Moms must not forget to spend time with their sons and their son's friends. Boys need to know that even with the demands of our jobs that they are important and that we enjoy their company. Become the coolest Mom on the block. Take your son, and even his friends and:

- Plant a garden.

- Head to a skate rink.

- Go bowling.

- Host a marble match.

- Have a tailgate party.

- Explore a nature center.

- Hike through the woods.

- Plan a Frisbee® tournament.

- Play a round of miniature golf.

- Find a climbing wall and climb it.

- Go fishing before the sun comes up.

- Tour the ultimate auto store and browse.

- Pick up and take out food and head to a park.

- Collect wood scraps and build—whatever.

- Buy earplugs and head to a concert featuring your son's favorite music group.

- Put on your swimsuit and have a water fight.

- Build a model wooden boat and sail it on a lake.

- Order pizza and have it delivered to you at the park or pool.

- Set up the croquet set at a park or on your front lawn.

- Pop the corn, settle in, and watch the Indianapolis 500.

- Make a map, hide the treasures, and watch them search.

- Window shop at a sporting goods store and create a wish list.

- Be lazy together, rent an old movie, and conclude the evening with a pillow fight.

- Go for a bike ride together.

- See who can make the best sand sculpture at the beach.

- Pick a sunny day to wash the family vehicle.

- Make a snowman.

- Visit a local museum.

- Make homemade pizza with your favorite toppings.

- Listen to a Christian comedian such as Mark Lowry.

- Go to a baseball game and start "the wave."

Chapter Five
Fun Ways to Worship

Worship is not meant to be an event or activity but a lifestyle. It's not implementing the routines of a religious ritual but an outpouring of the love of God in and through our lives. It's an act of our will, an expression of our emotions, and a means to communicate with God.

Besides sitting side-by-side in a church pew, how can a family worship together? What are the ingredients of worship? How can we teach our children to seek God's face, to praise His name, and adore our Savior? How can worship become an experience rather than a ritual?

Worship can become real to our children. In fact, it can become as real as going to a baseball game. The crowd cheers, raw emotions are shown, and the anticipation of something great is about to happen surges through your body. The teams show up, the game is played, and when it's time to leave, there's no doubt you've experienced an incredible event.

Our families can also share in worship experiences. We can sing together, praise God, and with enthusiasm, celebrate the good news of Jesus. We can kneel together and confess our sins knowing that the blood of Jesus is the ultimate sacrifice cleansing us from all wrongs. We can experience God's everlasting love and forgiveness. Our children can experience the presence of God Almighty through worship and embrace worship as a lifestyle.

Taste and See

God created us with five senses; sight, hearing, touch, smell, and taste. In the Old Testament the Israelite's worship included the use of all these senses to enrich and deepen their worship experience.

- Sight—What a marvelous and beautiful sight the colorful tabernacle was.

- Hearing—They beheld the music from the harp, lyre, and many other instruments.

- Touch—People offered sacrifices and blessings.

- Smell—There was incense and the aroma from the sacrifices burned as payment for sin.

- Taste—The bread was used as a holy offering to God. Food was symbolically used to remind the Israelites of God's provisions. It was the added touch to celebrations and the necessary ingredients of the feast.

Plan a time where you can incorporate these five senses into a worship experience for you and your family. Take your family where they can see God's beauty and listen to nature. Count the sounds you hear, the humming of a bird, rustling of grass, or the falling of a pinecone. Listen for God's still voice. Feel the breeze across your faces and feel the arms of a warm embrace as you offer each hug. Smell the aroma of the flowers, ocean, or trees. Taste and see that the Lord is good as you worship together.

Remember When

Symbols are an important aspect of worship. In Exodus 16:32 Moses said, *"This is what the LORD has commanded: 'Take an omer of manna and keep it for the generations to come, so they can see the bread I gave you to eat in the desert when I brought you out of Egypt.'"*

Aaron followed this instruction and placed two quarts of the manna in a jar. This manna had been God's daily gift to the Israelites. It appeared on the ground each morning while they wandered in the desert. Manna was God's way of providing food and nutrition to those He loved. Preserving this manna in a jar was to be the Israelites constant reminder of God's care, provision, and love.

What object could your family place in a "Remember When" jar symbolizing God's faithfulness? What item would remind you of how God met your needs when He cared for you while in a desert or difficult time? How would placing this jar in a visible location in your home encourage your family members in their daily walk with God?

Gather your family and ask each member to find an object that reminds him of God's provisions. Allow each family member to share the story their object represents and then have them place their item in the jar.

When our family filled our "Remember When" jar, we laughed as we knew no one else would understand why we had a jar sitting on  our table containing a Hot Wheels® car, a pencil, a baseball, a plastic bag filled with laundry soap, and a rock. You see God had been faithful to us. He had provided us with a new car and met our needs of transportation. He had provided fabulous teachers for our children. He had helped Jason through the ball season. He had cared for all our needs—even a broken washing machine. He had been our strength.

Another family took the "Remember When" jar to the next level. Vanessa's family had a great idea. Each time they experienced God's blessings and provision they placed a coin in a jar. Week after week they began to see how rich they truly are. You too, can be reminded of how God has cared for you. Gather your family, dust off an old jar, and remember when.

Up, Up, and Away

Another aspect of the worship experience is surrender. Teaching our children to surrender their worries and problems to God is vital and pleasing to Him. Matthew 6:25, 27, 34 states, *"Therefore I tell you, do not worry about your life. . .Who of you by worrying can add a single hour to his life? . . . Therefore do not worry about tomorrow for tomorrow will worry about itself. Each day has enough trouble of its own."* We are instructed to surrender, to hand our worries over to God, and to allow Him to handle, fix, and take care of our concerns. *"Cast your cares on the LORD and he will sustain you; he will never let the righteous fall."* (Psalm 55: 22)

But how can we teach our children to surrender, to cast their worries upon God? How can we help them release their cares to the One Who is faithful?

Years ago, our children were faced with concerns much too great for their little hearts to bear. From the deaths of beloved family members to their Uncle Rusty's being on the front lines in the Gulf War, their concerns were real. Marty and I sought ways in which we could use a hands-on experience to teach our children how to release their concerns to God. For Philippians 4:6 encourages us. *"Do not be anxious about anything, but in everything, by prayer and petition, with thanksgiving, present your requests to God."*

While the children gathered for family night, Marty headed for the closet and gathered the helium balloons. I met him with the marking pens and together we joined our children.

We began our family night in the usual fashion, thanking God for this time and for our family. Then Marty began to remind our children of the loving, caring, and all-powerful God in Whom we believed. He reminded them of how God had been faithful to Moses, Noah, David—and to us. "God is never going to stop caring for us," Marty said. "He can be trusted. We can depend upon Him to be with Uncle Rusty."

After Marty's reminders, we then handed each child a balloon and a permanent marking pen. Within moments they were each writing or drawing pictures representing their concerns. One balloon burst in the process. After the initial shock and laughter it brought, I gave Jenna another balloon. Soon the balloons took on a new look as the children's uncertainties were now scrawled across them.

"Let's go," Marty said standing up and heading to the door. With balloons in hand, each of us followed Marty outside where it was still light. He again restated his message of God's faithfulness and then gave the children their instructions. "I want you each to take your balloon's string and hold it in your hand. "Squeeze it! Hold it tight. Tighter! Can you feel your hand begin to hurt?"

The children nodded and answered "Yeah. It hurts. How much longer do we need to do this?"

"As long as you want to," Marty replied. "You see it's your choice. Just as it is your choice to trust God and give your worries to Him. We can decide right now. We can put Uncle Rusty in God's hands and give God this big worry." We wanted them to experience holding onto something tight and then feel the release as they set it free.

Something happened in those next few moments as our children relaxed their hands and released their balloons (away from all power lines.) Just as the balloons had been set free, they too had been set free from the pain of holding onto their worries. They experienced what it meant to let go and cast their cares upon God, (Psalm 55:22) and understood that He would take care of them. This truly was a worship experience.

I'm a Servant

It was the night before Jesus' death and He spent it with His disciples giving them their last minute instructions. Before He prepared and served the disciples the Passover feast, He showed them the importance of having a servant's heart. Jesus fastened a towel around His waist and then filled a washbasin with water and began to wash the disciples' feet. After Peter debated and insisted that Jesus would never wash his feet, Jesus convinced Peter and the other disciples that not only would He wash their feet, but they in turn were to wash the feet of those they served. *"Now that I, your Lord and Teacher, have washed your feet. You also should wash one another's feet. I have set you an example that you should do as I have done for you."* (John 13:14-15)

We can follow Jesus' instructions and example by teaching our children the importance of servanthood. The foot washing ceremony is an excellent way of hands-on learning. Fill a basin, bucket, or large bowl with water. Grab a few towels and some aprons. Gather your family and share with them the story found in John chapter thirteen. Then, one by one, take turns washing and drying each other's feet. Even with no tickling allowed, giggles may occur, and yet by the end of your time together, your family will have humbled themselves, served each other, and can anticipate the promised blessing as stated in John 13:17. *"Now that you know these things, you will be blessed if you do them."*

Experience a Sabbath

In the Old Testament, the Israelites were instructed to set aside the Sabbath for a day of worship, rest, and time to reflect on God's love and provision. This was a day that all work stopped, daily routines changed, and the Israelites worshiped and rested.

Our families too, need a sabbath. We need a day to set aside our to-do list, ball schedule, and daily routines—to teach the important. Schedule a sabbath, an entire day dedicated to worship, family, and reflection upon God; His majesty and provision. Attend a church service; go on a picnic to the park, head for the beach, or the plains. Be observant of nature and all that God created. Know that this holy day was created for you—to rest, be restored, and refreshed.

Stepping Out in Faith

Can you imagine the emotions the Israelites felt as they stood and faced the Jordan River? With its banks overflowing and their enemies on their trail, they took steps of faith, conquered their fears, obeyed God's commands, and stepped out into the water.

God kept His promises. He had been with the Israelites as they had wandered through the wilderness, fled from their enemies, and now stood safely on the other side. Joshua 4:1 states, *"When the whole nation had finished crossing the Jordan, the LORD said to Joshua, "Choose twelve men from among the people, one from each tribe, and tell them to take up twelve stones from the middle of the Jordan from right where the priests stood and to carry them over with you and put them down at the place where you stay tonight."*

Joshua did this and then explained to the Israelites that these stones were *"to serve as a sign among you. In the future, when your children ask you, 'What do these stones mean?' tell them that the flow of the Jordan was cut off before the ark of the covenant of the LORD. When it crossed the Jordan, the waters of the Jordan were cut off. Theses stones are to be a memorial to the people of Israel forever."* (Joshua 4:6-7)

No doubt, the Israelites would never forget the day they crossed the Jordan River, but God wanted them to have a constant reminder of Who parted the waters. Yes, twelve stones are what God used to provide a hands-on lesson for the Israelites and their children. Their parents were reminded to tell them not to be afraid of stepping out and following God's leading. These parents told their children how they saw no solution to their incredible dilemma—yet God had a plan.

Your family too can build a memorial as an act of worship. Have each member of your family gather a few stones from your yard or take a family field trip through the woods and find the perfect rocks. Then plan a time to meet together. Once there, take turns sharing situations from your lives depicting God's faithfulness and His awesome provision. Be bold and dare to share situations in your lives where you know you must step out in faith and walk towards your Jordan River. By being vulnerable and sharing (appropriate) life challenges, your children will learn how to live out their faith. By speaking of God's past faithfulness, you'll bring them hope and God's promises of today. By making a memorial—your family will never forget.

♥ Forty Days of Truth

As a family, commit to reading one chapter from the Bible together for the next forty days. (Choose a translation that is best suited to the ages of your children.) Whether it's before school, at dinner, or right before bed, gather your family and read. If by chance you miss a day, pick up where you left off and continue on. Don't let one missed day stop you from reaching your goal. See what happens when a family hears God's Word on a daily basis. Observe the truths from Hebrews 4:12, *"For the word of God is living and active. Sharper than any double-edged sword, it penetrates even to dividing soul and spirit, joints and marrow; it judges the thoughts and attitudes of the heart."*

Through your forty day commitment, witness the surgery God performs on your family. Watch the life-changing power of how His Word convicts, molds, heals, motivates, and touches your family. The Derby family suggests keeping a notebook available for family members to jot down their daily thoughts, and record and share God's Word in action. The journal can be shared with your family each night at your weekly family night or at the end of your forty days.

Time on Our Knees

King David in the Old Testament was fully human. He loved God and yet at times he chose to sin. David experienced the consequences that his sin brought and also the agony and distress of living with unconfessed sin. He also knew the blessing of a restored relationship with God and the precious gift of forgiveness.

Throughout the Old Testament, we read how worship included the confession of one's sins and sacrifices as payment for these sins. The children were taught by their parent's example, how to maintain a pure and right relationship with God (see Genesis 22 and Leviticus 9).

We too, can share this worship experience. Claim the promise found in 1 John 1:9: *"If we confess our sins, he is faithful and just and will forgive us our sins and purify us from all unrighteousness."* Kneel together as a family and confess your sins. Teach your children that the blood of Jesus is the ultimate sacrifice, cleansing you from all wrongs. Show them by your example how to confess and experience God's forgiveness and restoration. Sing together, praise God, and with enthusiasm, celebrate Jesus—the One who made your forgiveness possible.

Dedicate Your Home

In the Old Testament, people, places, and objects were often dedicated to God. This meant that they were set apart for a special purpose. For example, in 2 Chronicles 7:4-5 King Solomon and his people dedicated the Temple to God declaring it a place of worship.

Your family can choose to dedicate your home to God, offering it to Him for His glory. You can come together and thank Him for your house and its comforts. Ask Christ to dwell in each room, keeping all who enter and depart safe. Then declare your home to be a place of worship, praise, unity, peace, and love.

 Make a Mezuzah

A mezuzah is an encased parchment scroll that is placed on the right doorpost of the entrance of rooms in Jewish homes. The scroll is inscribed with two Biblical passages (Deuteronomy 6:4-9 and 11:13-21). On the back side of the parchment the name *Shaddai*—which means *Almighty*, is written. The paper is rolled up from left to right so that *Shaddai* is visible.

Before affixing the mezuzah to a doorpost, a blessing is recited. In Jewish households, the mezuzah is positioned on the doorpost at an angle, one-third of the way down. The mezuzah is a constant reminder of God's love and protection, and the responsibilities each has to his faith. It is customary upon entering or leaving a Jewish home to touch the mezuzah by first putting your finger tips to your lips and then touching the mezuzah which acknowledges God's holiness and protection, and is a reminder to keep God's word in your heart and on your lips.

Read Deuteronomy 6:5-9 and 11:13-21, and have your family make their own mezuzah. Bless your family by partaking in the richness of Jewish tradition. Hang your mezuzah from the doorframe of your home. You, too, will be reminded to keep God's Word on your mind and in your heart.

Conduct a Walkthrough

Take your family on a tour of your home. Stop in each room and say a prayer committing the room to the Lord for His purposes. A simple prayer (below) may be recited by a "leader" and then repeated by other family members.

God, we consecrate this room to You. We set it a part and ask that it be used for Your glory. We ask that You bless it and make it a holy dwelling place. In Jesus name, we pray, Amen.

Once each room has been dedicated, gather your family for a time of worship. Each family member who is able can read a portion of Scripture. Suggested scriptures are: Hebrews 3:4, Deuteronomy 6:5-9, and Psalm 15. Choose a few songs and sing them unto the Lord. One of our favorites for this situation is "Me and My House" by Tim Sheppard © 1981.

You can end your time together with another prayer. A prayer that you could use is:

"God Almighty, we thank You for our home. May our actions, words, and lives honor You as we dwell in it. May it be filled with praise. May strangers find friendship, may people find healing, may we all experience Your peace. As Psalm 84 resounds, "How lovely is Your dwelling place, O LORD Almighty!"

Once this prayer is complete, the leader can end the dedication by saying:

"Now, may God watch over you when you come and when you go, now and forever, Amen."

Shout to the Lord

Children are full of expression. They giggle when something strikes them funny; they wave their arms to catch a friend's attention, and cheer with gusto. Somehow while growing up, we tend to lose the freedom to express ourselves and become more reserved.

Let's think about it, God is Almighty. He alone is the creator of the universe—the breath that gave us life. Yet how do we worship Him? Do we as children use our entire bodies to express our joy and thanks? At what point do we bow down to show honor, make requests, and intercede for others? What tone is in our voice and how do we give God thanks and exalt His name? Gather your children for family night and celebrate Jesus. Clap your hands, rejoice with cheers, and shout praises to the Lord. Be like David and dance before Him with joy. Grab your trumpet and play like Gideon. Act like Moses and Aaron and sing up to the heavens, or be a Daniel and kneel before Him. End your worship time with reading from Psalm 150. And yes, *Let everything that has breath praise the LORD."* (verse 6)

Chapter Six
Fun and Faith

As Christian parents it's our desire that our children become grounded in their faith—knowing what they believe in and in Whom they believe. Through fun, faith can be enriched, lessons can be taught, and lives can be changed. Through faith and fun, your family can "*abound more and more in the knowledge and depth of insight, so that you may be able to discern what is best and may be pure and blameless until the day of Christ.*" (Philippians 1:9)

Psalm 119:105 tells us that God's Word is a lamp unto our feet and a light for our paths. Exposing our children to this light is a God-given responsibility. Together, by their side, we can walk this path and follow the light and have a great time doing so.

One way to encourage your children to explore God's Word is through creating a game such as Bible Pop-Up. Grab a pen, some index cards, and your Bible. I suggest using a Life Application® Bible by Zondervan Publishers, or a Bible with footnotes, references, and a commentary. Read the portion of Scripture that you desire to share with your children. You may want to begin with one of the Gospels and read chapter by chapter, or you may want to select a specific Bible character or story.

 ## Bible Pop-Up

Once you've read the Scripture, ask yourself, "What happened in this story? How did God intervene and show His faithfulness? What life lessons were taught?" After you've answered these questions, ask the Lord to bless you as you use your creativity and think up questions, creating a game pertaining to the portion of Scripture you read. Write one question on the front of each index card.

Then underneath the question, provide the answer to the question and two alternatives that are incorrect—similar to a multiple-choice question. This will allow your children to think, ponder, and select their answer. The correct answer can be placed on the backside of each card.

Here is an example how the game can be played:

1. Read the Scripture selected.

2. Deem one person as the leader and have her read the question.

3. After the entire question has been read, the first family member to pop-up to his feet or raise his hand, has the opportunity to answer the question. If he answers correctly, he gets a point. If the question is answered incorrectly, the family member sits down and the next person to stand or raise her hand gets a chance to answer correctly.

On the following pages are Bible Pop-Up sample questions that pertain to the story of Noah and the Ark. These questions can be used as examples as you study the Scripture and create question cards of your own. Note that the story of Noah and the Ark is covered in Genesis chapters six through nine. These chapters can be broken up and not all read at one sitting.

Use the Bible Pop-Up questions that pertain to the portion of Scripture that you have read. Save these questions and add them to your question cards, and play Bible Pop-Up anytime you wish.

Remember, a family who plays together can also pray together. A family who incorporates faith and fun in their home is blessed.

Through exciting and unique activities, our children can hear God's Word and let it penetrate into their hearts. By going to fun places with family and friends, our families can truly live well, laugh often, love much, and give God the glory.

Bible Pop-Up Questions
(based on Genesis 6:1-9:17)

1. The story of Noah begins by telling us that *"The Lord saw how great man's wickedness on the earth had become . . ."* It also says, *"The Lord was grieved that he had made man on the the earth, and his heart was filled with_____."*

    a. Fury
    b. Pain
    c. Rage

2. What type of wood did God tell Noah to use to build the ark?

    a. Maple
    b. Cypress
    c. Pine

3. Why did God choose to save Noah and his family from the flood?

    a. Noah walked with God.
    b. Noah had the largest family.
    c. God knew that Noah had flood insurance.

4. What were the names of Noah's three sons?

    a. Shem, Ham, and Japheth
    b. Shadrach, Meshach, and Abednego
    c. Adam, Cain, and Abel

5. What did God ask Noah to do?

    a. Go to Nineveh
    b. Lead the Israelites out of bondage
    c. Build an ark

Bible Pop-Up Questions
(based on Genesis 6:1-9:17)

6. God gave Noah blueprints—specific instructions for how to build the ark. The large boat was to be 450 feet long, 75 feet wide, and _____ feet high.

   a. 33 feet
   b. 45 feet
   c. Too many to count.

7. The ark was no canoe. God instructed Noah to build it _____ stories high.

   a. Two: one sun deck and one deck for sleeping
   b. One: a single deck for animals and Noah's family
   c. Three: a lower, middle and upper deck

8. How would Noah and his family get air to breathe while living on the ark?

   a. Through a sunroof
   b. Through a door
   c. Noah was not worried as the ark did not have a roof.

9. How did the animals get onto the ark?

   a. The animals would come to Noah.
   b. Noah captured them.
   c. Noah's sons chased them down.

10. How many birds went into the ark?

   a. Several
   b. A family of four
   c. Two: one male and one female

Bible Pop-Up Questions
(based on Genesis 6:1-9:17)

11. How old was Noah when God sent the flood?

    a.   452 years old
    b.   200 years old
    c.   600 years old

12. God sent the rain for_____?

    a.   400 days
    b.   44 days
    c.   40 days and 40 nights

13. Once Noah, his wife, their sons, their wives, and the animals were on the ark, who shut its mighty door?

    a.   The Lord
    b.   Noah
    c.   Noah's three strong sons

14. After being in the ark 47 days, Noah opened the ark's window and set out a dove. What did this dove bring back to the ark?

    a.   A fig leaf
    b.   An olive leaf
    c.   A bright, red strawberry

15. How did Noah know when it was time for him and his family to leave the ark?

    a.   They were restless.
    b.   Noah's sons were seasick.
    c.   God told Noah it was time to come out of the ark.

Bible Pop-Up Questions
(based on Genesis 6:1-9:17)

16. Once Noah's family and all the animals were off the ark, Noah
    _____.

     a.   Built an altar to God
     b.   Took a week vacation
     c.   Held a party

17. God made a promise to Noah and his sons—a covenant for all
    generations. This covenant said that never again would God
    allow a flood to destroy the earth. What did God send as a sign
    of this promise?

     a.   Three Wise Men
     b.   A rainbow
     c.   40 days of sunshine

18. One lesson from Noah's life is_____.

     a.   God is faithful to those who obey Him.
     b.   Plan ahead for a rainy day.
     c.   Learn to swim.

Bible Pop-Up Answers
(based on Genesis 6:1-9:17)

1. b. Pain
   "The LORD was grieved that he had made man on the earth, and his heart was filled with pain." (Genesis 6:6)

2. b. Cypress
   "So make yourself an ark of cypress wood . . ." (Genesis 6:14)

3. a. Noah walked with God.
   "Noah was a righteous man, blameless among the people of his time, and he walked with God." (Genesis 6:9)

4. a. Shem, Ham, and Japheth
   "Noah had three sons: Shem, Ham and Japheth." (Genesis 6:10)

5. c. Build an ark
   "So make yourself an ark . . ." (Genesis 6:14)

6. b. 45 feet
   "This is how you are to build it: The ark is to be 450 feet long, 75 feet wide and 45 feet high." (Genesis 6:15)

7. c. Three: a lower, middle, and upper deck
   ". . . and make lower, middle and upper decks." (Genesis 6:16)

8. b. Through a door
   "Put a door in the side of the ark. . . ." (Genesis 6:16)

9. a. The animals would come to Noah.
   ". . . every kind of creature that moves along the ground will come to you to be kept alive." (Genesis 6:20)

10. c. Two: one male and one female
    "You are to bring into the ark two of all living creatures, male and female . . . Two of every kind of bird . . ." (Genesis 6:19-20)

Bible Pop-Up Answers
(based on Genesis 6:1-9:17)

11. c. 600 years old
    "Noah was six hundred years old when the floodwaters came on the earth." (Genesis 7:6)

12. c. 40 days and 40 nights
    "And rain fell on the earth forty days and forty nights." (Genesis 7:12)

13. a. The Lord
    *"The animals going in were male and female of every living thing, as God had commanded Noah. Then the L*ORD* shut him in."* (Genesis 7:16)

14. b. An olive leaf
    "When the dove returned to him in the evening, there in its beak was a freshly plucked olive leaf! Then Noah knew that the water had receded from the earth." (Genesis 8:11)

15. c. God told Noah it was time to come out of the ark.
    "Then God said to Noah, "Come out of the ark, you and your wife and your sons and their wives." (Genesis 8:15-16)

16. a. Built an altar to God
    *"Then Noah built an altar to the L*ORD* and, taking some of all the clean animals and clean birds, he sacrificed burnt offerings on it."* (Genesis 8:20)

17. b. A rainbow
    "I have set my rainbow in the clouds, and it will be the sign of the covenant between me and the earth." (Genesis 9:13)

18. a. God is faithful to those who obey Him.
    *"The L*ORD* preserves the faithful. . . ."* (Psalm 31:23)

Discussion Questions for Genesis 6:9-9:17

1. Despite how impossible the task appeared, Noah received his instructions from God, obeyed, and began building. Do you think that it was easy for Noah to obey God?

2. The ark's estimated length was 450 feet. What would you say to God if He asked you to take on such a task?

3. Do you think that others teased Noah and his family while they worked so diligently building the boat? If so, how do you think Noah and his family felt?

4. God took care of the details and rounded up all the animals while Noah obeyed and built the ark. What details are you trusting God to take care of in your life?

5. One lesson from Noah's life is God's faithfulness to those who obey Him. Are there areas in your life where you need to be more faithful and trusting in God?

6. When Noah and his family got out of the ark, they saw what the Earth looked like after being hit by the flood. What do you think the Earth looked like then?

7. God chose to save Noah from the flood because he was a righteous and blameless man who had a personal relationship with Him. Which of these characteristics do you posses? Which characteristics do you admire? Are there any you aspire for your own life?

Discussion Questions for Genesis 6:9-9:17

8. The Bible states that at the time Noah was living on the Earth, mankind's actions were evil and corrupt. To put an end to the corruption, God decided to destroy them. If you could travel back to warn the people, what would you say to help them live a life that was pleasing to God?

9. How do you think Noah's sons, Shem, Ham, and Japheth felt knowing they would never see their friends again? Have you ever had to leave a friend behind?

10. After the flood ended, God promised He would never allow a flood to destroy the Earth. Can you recall other promises that God has given us?